The A-Z Basketball Book

*What Every Player Needs to Know
to Be <u>Great</u> at the Game!*

Gary Pluff

Upcentral Publishing
29 Braeside Road,
Baldwinsville, New York 13027

Ordering Information:
Quantity sales. Special discounts are available on quantity purchases by corporations, associations, teams, and others. For details, contact the publisher at the address above.

ISBN-10: 0989746615
ISBN-13: 978-0-9897466-1-8
Upcentral Publishing, Baldwinsville, NY 13027

DEDICATION

For my Mom and Dad; without your love and guidance this wouldn't be possible. For my awesome family; Christi, Casey and Calli, you guys are the best and the light of my life. And for the dreamers and those that dare to be great-no effort ever goes unrewarded.

Table of Contents

ACKNOWLEDGMENTS

Special thanks to Cheri Yuco, Chris Jarvis, and Judy Bullard for their unselfish help with making this happen. Thank you to my beautiful daughter Calli and her keen eye. And to "me boy" Casey, and all his "buds," for helping out with the videos that supplement this book.

INTRODUCTION

When growing up most kids dream of being great at something. But in order to be great at something you first have to have knowledge of what it takes to be great. That's what this book is all about. It's the 40 years of what I've learned from playing, coaching, watching, and studying the game that I love, all packed into one book.

What's required of you is to take the knowledge and do something with it. And if you do that, I still can't completely guarantee you will become a great player. Maybe you won't work hard enough to master all the skills of the game required to be great. Or maybe you will have physical limitations that end up holding you back. But what I CAN guarantee is that, if you don't know and understand the information in this book, AND work hard at the game, you will never be a great basketball player! That's how life works. Life is about educating yourself to achieve success and working very hard at it.

I suggest you first read the book all the way through one time and then keep it handy to refer back to over and over again. That's what it will take to really understand all that's written here. After that, it's up to you to put in the hard work, discipline, and dedication that are needed to be a great player.

The A-ZBasketballBook.com website is also there to help you along your path towards greatness. It has instructional videos featuring fundamental skills and drills and lots of other basketball information that I will continue to add to and update.

So keep dreaming big, work hard, and always continue to believe in yourself! And very importantly, enjoy the process of achieving greatness! That means you have to have fun with it all. Have fun not only with the pickup games and the shooting around, but also with all the hard work that has to be put into the sport in order to be great at it.

So are you ready? Let's begin with the letter "A."

A

Attitude
Anticipate
Assert
Assist
Achieve
Adversity

Attitude

The number one character trait required for success in anything is a great attitude. And your attitude is the one thing you can control even when things aren't going well. It's important to maintain a strong positive attitude both mentally and in the way you carry yourself on the court-your body language. Expect the best and be optimistic and carry yourself in a strong confident manner. From day to day there will be lots of times when your attitude is tested in many different ways. It could be when you're having a bad game or get bad calls from the referees or when negative people try to cut you down. These are the times to NOT drop your shoulders, mope, or argue calls, and whine and complain. Save the sour looking face and the flailing arms and all the ranting and raving for the lesser players with bad attitudes. That is not you! You will continue to play on in a strong confident manner believing that things will turn around. And things will turn around for you, if you maintain your great attitude and your positive body language. It's real easy to have a great attitude when things are going well. The test will be how you act and how you think when things aren't going your way. Act the best. Expect the best. Be the best. Maintain a great attitude and project strong, confident body language at all times!

Anticipate

Anticipate means to think ahead about what you believe is going to happen on the court before it actually happens. You can't always just wait for something to happen and then react to it. Basketball is a very fast game and all the great players have great attitudes and constantly anticipate what they think is going to happen while they're on the court. You have to think ahead to where you think the ball will bounce off the rim or where a player will pass the ball or where the screen is coming from before it actually happens. Think for a minute about how you would walk through a rain forest with lots of dangerous animals lurking all around you. If you wanted to "win" which in this case means surviving the dangerous jungle, you would have to be on "high alert" and would have to be constantly thinking and anticipating what might happen. If you failed to do this, then the moment you let your guard down is when a big jaguar would leap out and throw down a huge dunk on you! Be mentally sharp and be sure to anticipate the action the <u>whole entire time</u> you are on the basketball court.

Assert

Assert means you have to impose what you want to have happen upon your opponents. You have to have a great attitude and the confidence and courage to assert your vision. You can't be laid back just being a part of what is going on around you and hope good things will happen. Have an assertive, positive attitude. Expect success. Be aware of what is going on around you and anticipate the action before it happens! Attitude – Anticipate – Assert!

Assist

I'm sure you know that an assist is when a teammate passes the ball to another teammate which leads directly to a score. Assisting, like proper rebounding, is severely lacking in youth basketball today. The majority of players want to dribble and shoot the ball. The great players are the players that can dribble and shoot, but are also very aware that the ball needs to be given up in order for their team to be successful. We live in a "me, me" society where too many people are only thinking of themselves. This mentality shows itself quite often on the basketball court. The player that is only thinking about scoring and dribbling is far too common in youth basketball. It's important for you to understand the existence of an unchanging and very powerful force in the world that's referred to as a "universal law." It applies to all of life as well as to basketball. And here it is-**as you give you get**. That's right. As you give you get! As a young person this is pretty hard to understand. I'm sure you're thinking that you want all the best for yourself. This is natural. But what you have to understand is that, when you help others, you benefit yourself. Good things will happen when you give! Basketball is a team sport and you win or lose as a team. Through the years I've seen a lot of talented high scoring players on losing teams. If you want to win both in life and in basketball, you have got to think of others. Be unselfish and look to set your teammates up for scores. If you are a good shooter and scorer you will score and the points will come in the natural flow of things. You don't have to hog the ball and force shots. If you do, your teammates will not want to pass you the ball because THEY will want to take their turn to score. This is when team chemistry breaks down and you will lose. Because you were selfish and thinking only of yourself you become a loser. If you are thinking of your teammates and giving of yourself for the betterment of the team, the ball will come back into your hands and you will have all the opportunities you desire. You will help your team win and you will become a winner! Magic Johnson the great Los Angeles Laker guard was a master at understanding this concept. Make others around you better. Understand the importance of assists. Give and you will get!

Achieve

Achievement is what you will be rewarded with when you read, learn, and put into practice all that is in this book. Achievement in anything will not come until you understand what must be done AND then do it! You have to read, understand, and then put into practice all that is discussed here. There is a lot of information and a lot to learn, so it is important to keep this handy and re-read all the different letters of the alphabet often. It's one thing to really know all the information covered here, which will take time, but it is quite another thing to put it into practice.

Adversity

Adversity is a fact of life and so it is with the game of basketball. You can know and do the right things and you will still face hardships, difficulties, and misfortunes in life. There's no avoiding having to overcome adversity. A great quote, which has had a big impact on my life, is, "It's not so much what happens to you in life, but how you respond to what happens to you." Think about that for a moment and remember that quote when adversity comes knocking. This is a very powerful notion. We get to choose from our own free will how we will respond in any given situation! The power lies within you! If you understand the quote and are truly striving for greatness, you will look inward and know the right things to do when faced with adversity.

Summary

To summarize what has been learned from the letter "A" I hope that you understand that the achievement or success that you seek is the result (or byproduct) of knowing and doing the right things correctly and consistently, over time (also known as being disciplined). Will you have a great attitude when the chips are down? Will you consistently assert your will on your opponent and stay mentally sharp and focused working on anticipating what is happening on the court? Will you understand the importance of assists, be unselfish with the basketball, and look to set your teammates up for shots? Will you be wise enough to overcome adversity when it arises? You need to learn and put into practice these and many more parts of the game in order to be a great player.

Have a positive attitude, anticipate what is going on around you, assert your will on your opponent, always be looking to dish a sweet assist, and understand that achievement will not come until you put these and many more things to be discussed into your game. So are you ready to read, learn, and put into practice all the rest of the pieces of the puzzle needed for basketball greatness? Let's get on with it!

<u>B</u>

Ball handling
Boxing out

Ball handling

There is no substitute for having great ball handling skills. You have to have them! Practice in your basement, in your garage, and if your parents let you, do drills in the kitchen! You don't need to have access to a basketball court to become a good dribbler. Do it anywhere and do it often. Not having great handles in basketball is like a hockey player not knowing how to skate! Many great ball handling drills to learn from are on my A-ZBasketballBook.com website. They start from basic drills and move onto much more advanced drills. Practice them all as much as possible. Very little space is needed. If you can't get outdoors, hopefully you can practice in your garage, basement, or at a local gym. If you're going to be great at basketball you have to be a great ball handler. Use my website and the many other online resources available to learn drills and practice often.

Boxing out

Most players know what boxing out is, but very few actually do it! Boxing out is a very aggressive and physical skill. To correctly box out means you not only block out your opponent when getting a rebound, but you also move your opponent backwards. My experience with youth coaching is that a very low percentage of players actually do this. So let's get this right. Here are the steps to boxing out: 1) When a player shoots the ball, or better yet, when you think a shot is about to go up (anticipate) look for a player on the other team. 2) Get low in an athletic position and step in front of them, while keeping them behind you with your arms. 3) Trap them behind you with your arms while staying very low. The power needs to come from your legs, and you need to make contact with your rear, back, and arms. 4) Move them forcefully backwards. As you are doing this, try to pick up where the ball is and go after it. The key here; this is VERY IMPORTANT, is to not just watch the basketball when a shot is taken. YOU MUST FIRST LOOK FOR A PERSON TO BOX OUT!! Go after the ball, only after you have completed the four steps explained above and you have your opponent boxed out. If you can do this, you will put yourself in the top 10% of all youth basketball players.

Boxing out properly is a very important part of basketball and one that coaches love to see players do. You can make it hard for your coach to take you out of the game, if you are boxing out every time a shot is taken!

<u>C</u>

Character
Confidence
Conditioning
Commitment
Contact
Competition

Character/Confidence

The combination of qualities and features that make up a person are known as their character. You want to have positive character traits by doing the right things both on and off the court. Play hard, but play fair. Help an opposing player up from the court. Have confidence in yourself and set high standards for yourself. Speak the truth. Stand up for what you know is right. How will this make you a better basketball player? When you have strong moral character you are a confident person. When you are committed to doing what you know should be done and what needs to be done, you will not only feel good about yourself and be confident, but others will also look up to you. You will be looked upon as a person that has strong character and confidence. Your teammates will trust you and look up to you.

Conditioning

There is no substitution for conditioning. You have to be in top physical condition. You need to set a routine that is going to improve your cardiovascular endurance and increase your strength and speed. You can increase your strength by doing a lot of push-ups and dips and should also do core work like abdominal crunches, leg lifts, and lower back extensions. In the early part of your teen years, you can eventually move on to weights. This strength work needs to be combined with running. You absolutely need to run for at least 20 minutes, at least four times a week, to increase your leg strength and improve your cardiovascular endurance. To improve your speed you need to run sprints. You have to be committed to running for distance, running for speed, and working on your strength in order to become a great basketball player. You also need to stretch as often as possible both before working out and after working out. Stretching is very important as it allows muscles to work properly and will also help you to avoid injury when competing. Your conditioning program does not have to be long or complicated, but you do need to work a routine into and around all your basketball training and playing in order to become a great player.

Commitment/Confidence

To stick with a regularly scheduled conditioning program takes strong character and commitment. You are doing what you know needs to be done. When you are committed to what you know is right and true, you will not only have strong character, but you will have confidence in yourself. You will not achieve your best at basketball without character, conditioning, commitment, and confidence. You can see how they all go hand in hand.

Contact

Basketball is a contact sport. You cannot be afraid of taking on contact in a basketball game. Contact is necessary to box out, to draw a charge, to fight through screens, to get a loose ball, and for many other aspects of basketball. When you have strong character, are in great condition, and are committed and confident, you will have no problem being physical and taking on contact. It is a very important part of the sport and you have to be willing to give and receive contact. You will not escape it if you plan on playing basketball. It must be embraced and enjoyed. You'll get a few bumps and bruises, but that's the nature of the game! The bumps and bruises will heal. Knowing you didn't give it your best will linger for a long time. If you want to be the best player you are capable of becoming, embrace the fact that basketball is a contact sport!

Competition

You should never worry about the competition or fear the competition. Always respect your opponent, but never overly concern yourself with who you're playing. In the end, we are all really competing with ourselves. It's all about self-improvement and trying to be better than you were the day before. You will win some competitions and you will lose some. Enjoy the thought that you're going to bring the best of what you have to offer to the surface on that given day. Win with grace and lose with dignity. You can be a fierce and aggressive competitor and assert yourself to the best of your ability without getting angry or violent. Keep your emotions in check and enjoy the competition. Shake your opponents hand when the game is over. If you lose, there will be other competitions. If you win, be humble and graceful. Whatever the outcome is, you should always reflect on how well you and your team performed. There will be times when you played less than your best and won, and times when you and your team played great and lost. Either way, the sun will rise in the morning and you should reflect and learn from the game that was played. It's all part of enjoying your basketball journey.

<u>D</u>

Defense
Discipline
Determination
Dedication

Defense

Defense is one of the most important facets of basketball, if not the most important! You have to be in your best condition in order to play your best defense. To play your best defense takes total determination and dedication. You have to be determined and dedicated period! You can't half-commit; and you will half-commit if you are not in top physical condition and/or not dedicated and determined! A-ZBasketballBook.com has lots of defensive drills and techniques for you to learn from. Once they are learned, it's up to you to have the heart and will to dedicate yourself and have the determination to be a great defender.

Discipline

Discipline can be defined as, "Training expected to produce a specific character or pattern of behavior." If you truly want to be great at the game of basketball you have to be disciplined to do the right things at the right time, even when you don't feel like it. And do them to the best of your ability. You have to train yourself to produce a pattern of behavior that will lead to greatness. Don't expect someone else to do it for you. That's what discipline is; putting your strong character and commitment to work by doing what it takes consistently over time. The only way to ingrain and make this proper pattern of behavior a habit is to keep

The A-Z Basketball Book

doing the right things as well as you can over a long period of time. You have to be disciplined! No one else can do it for you.

Determination/Dedication

Hopefully you understand the importance of discipline and you also understand the "Cs" and have committed to a conditioning program. This will give you the tools you need to be able to play defense. Once you have the tools, you have to be determined and dedicated to play excellent defense. Defensive slides, closing out on a shooter, seeing man and ball, taking a charge; all of these defensive techniques and fundamentals can be taught by your coaches. What can't be taught is how to have heart. You've got to want it. As already mentioned, A-ZBasketballBook.com has information and drills to help you become a better defender. Once you know how to play proper defense, and you are working towards being in great condition, defense is about being 100% determined and dedicated to give it your all to impose your will on the offensive player. You must be relentlessly determined and dedicated to never let up. The majority of young players love to shoot and dribble and think that is what will get them recognized as being a good player and help them to stand out. Very few are committed and determined and have the discipline to dedicate themselves to play great defense. Those who

21

do will get recognized and stand out. There will always be a place on the court for the fiercely determined and dedicated defensive player. Coaches love that type of player, and if you want to be considered a great player, that player has to be you!

E

Excitement
Enthusiasm
Energy
Emotions
Endurance

Excitement/Enthusiasm/Energy

Excitement, enthusiasm, and energy go hand in hand. You have to bring these emotions with you into every practice and onto the court during games. Ralph Waldo Emerson said, "Nothing great could be accomplished without enthusiasm." You have to have excitement for the game. Be enthusiastic and play with high energy. There will be times when you feel flat and don't feel very excited or enthused. This is when you need to look inward and do some things to bring out your positive emotions. Clap loudly. Bounce up and down. Talk to your teammates and encourage them. Get your heart pumping and some energy flowing through you and around you. Working up energy and enthusiasm will help get you excited about the game again and it's contagious to everyone around you. Be the great player that brings the game to life by bringing high energy, enthusiasm, and excitement into every practice and into every game.

Emotions

While the game is going on, you don't want to become overly excited or dejected at any given time. I see too much of this in basketball today. You should keep your emotions in check when you are on the court. Play on. Do your celebrating after the game is over with. The great UCLA coach John Wooden felt very strongly about this. And as he usually was about most things, he was right.

Endurance

As you keep your emotions in check throughout the course of the game, you also must have the endurance to give it your all for the entire game. Endurance cannot be achieved without conditioning and playing a lot of basketball games. You have to be in game playing shape to have the endurance to give it your all from the opening tip to the game ending buzzer.

Summary

Be excited about the game and bring that excitement, enthusiasm, and energy into everything you do. Remember to keep your emotions in check and be sure that you commit to being in top physical condition so you will have the endurance to impose your will onto your opponent all the way to the final buzzer!

<u>F</u>

Fundamentals
Fight through screens
Focus
Faith

Fundamentals

There is no substitution for the fundamentals. You can play thousands of games and shoot thousands of shots, but if you don't have the proper fundamentals it will all lead to a dead end. You must understand the fundamentals of the game and commit yourself to a routine (like conditioning) of working on them. The fundamentals can be learned from coaches and online. They are endless. There are fundamentals of shooting, dribbling, passing, footwork, rebounding, and it goes on and on. Commit to a routine of working on the fundamentals and always be willing to learn more. Challenge yourself to continue to learn something new because there is always something new to learn. In life and in basketball, you must commit to constant and never-ending improvement. A commitment to learning the fundamentals of basketball is crucial to becoming the best player you are capable of becoming.

Fight through screens

Fighting through screens goes along with being willing to take on contact. You can't always just switch on screens. Sometimes the situation will warrant that you step over the top of the screen and be very physical to fight through the screen with determination. Do not defer! Basketball is a game of imposing your will. Fight and I mean FIGHT through a screen by stepping over the top and being physical and being willing to take on contact. It will help if you can anticipate that the screen is coming, which should be aided by a teammate loudly announcing that a screen is coming to your left or to your right. Be willing to fight through screens like your life depends on it. And yes, this will mean that you have to take on contact!

Focus

The only time that exists is the present. By that I mean that what happened in the past or what might happen in the future have nothing to do with the here and now. The present is all that matters. I know the future matters very much and is very important, but in basketball, as in life, when you have a task to perform you need to maintain a laser-like focus, be in the moment and perform that task to the best of your abilities. Don't think about what has already happened or what might happen. The only exception to this rule is when you visualize yourself succeeding at the task that you are about to undertake. (More on visualizing when we get to the letter "V.") Stay in the present. Listen and make eye contact with your coach. What your coach is saying is the most important thing in the world to you at that particular time. Don't look around the gym, or think about what you're going to do after practice or after the game. To stay focused takes a lot of discipline and self-control. Work on staying focused in each and every moment and perform your tasks to the best of your current abilities. (Be where you are with all you have.) Great players always stay focused and work very hard at doing so.

Faith

Whenever you set high goals for yourself and really put yourself out there to achieve at a high level, you are going to need to have faith. Faith is believing in yourself. Believe that when you commit to the process of doing something well, good things are going to happen. You will not always get immediate positive feedback for all your efforts, but you will need to continue to have faith and stick with it. Always keep your mind focused on each and every task at hand and perform them to the best of your ability. In the end, you may not become the greatest basketball player in the world, but striving to achieve your best will always be rewarded. Always work hard, play hard, stay focused, and keep the faith!

<u>G</u>

Goal setting
Get low
Go to the ball
Get back
Gratitude

Goal setting

The majority of anything worthwhile in life has been accomplished by setting goals. You start with a vision or a dream of what you would like to accomplish and set goals on how you are going to get there. When you are dedicating yourself to working out, try as much as possible to include concrete numbers. For example: I will lift X pounds of weights, X many times, for X amount of days of the week. Or, I will make X amount of shots, from all the different spots on the floor, X number of days a week. I will run X amount of days of the week, etc. Commit yourself as much as possible to concrete and measurable goals so that you will know whether you've done them or not. The world is littered with people with good intentions that let the days get by them because they never grounded their dreams with concrete, measureable goals.

Get low

"Get low" means you have to be down in an athletic position very often in basketball. Think of a shortstop fielding a ground ball or a skier going down a mountain or a tennis player in a position to return a serve. This is the position that you have to be in almost continuously in basketball. You will hear coaches say very frequently, "get your butt down." Many players get lazy and just will not get in an athletic position when they should be. It's the position you need to be in when you are looking to receive a pass, when you're fighting for a rebound, when you play defense, and when you're looking to shoot off the dribble. You have to get low! You have to get your butt down!! Why don't young players understand this? Can you imagine a tiger that is hungry getting ready to jump on a gazelle by standing up? To get from point A to point B quickly you have to first get in a crouch and off your heels to be able to spring into action. For you to be able to do that quickly in basketball you have to be low and in an athletic position to make good things happen. GET LOW!!

Go to the ball

You should always think about going toward the ball. For a lot of players this is instinct, but for other players it doesn't come so easy. Always remember to move towards the ball when it is passed to you. The defense will usually be coming hard to pick off a pass, and if you don't move towards the pass to receive it, there's a good chance the ball will be stolen. If you're away from the action and the ball is going out of bounds and there are players from both teams hustling to try to save it, never stand and watch. Always move towards the ball so you will have a chance at having it thrown to you. Anticipate where the ball will bounce off the rim and go get it! Always think about going to the ball!

Get back

Get back means that you have to GET BACK on defense as soon as there is a change of possession. If you get a pass stolen or miss a shot, and the opposing team gets the rebound, the first thing you need to be thinking about is getting back on defense. This means that you turn immediately and sprint all the way back down the court to the paint area and then turn around to find your man to guard. If the person you're guarding is jogging back on offense, and the ball is ahead of you up the court, you need to sprint up the court to help out your teammates. The person you're guarding is still getting up the court and is no threat to anyone, so why guard him? Leave him and sprint up the court to join in on the action. You can turn around and find him after you have sprinted up the court to help your teammates. If you want to be great at basketball, you have to understand that you have to get back on defense **immediately** after your team loses possession of the ball by sprinting all the way back to the paint area every single time.

Gratitude

Gratitude is a very important trait to have in life. We need to be grateful for what we have and not focus so much on what we wish we had. Too much of success today is measured by material goods. When you get into comparing what you have with others, it's a losing game. You need to be grateful for what you have right now. You may not have many material things but you still need to be appreciative and grateful for what you do have. There's an old proverb that sums this up nicely: "I once felt sorry for myself because I had no shoes until I met a man that had no feet." Be grateful for your sound mind and healthy body and the opportunity to live in a free country where you can work to become just about anything you want to become. Be grateful for the opportunity to play the great game of basketball and give thanks daily for the blessings you have. It's okay to work hard for more things that you want out of life, but always give thanks and be grateful for what you are already in possession of.

H

Head up
Hands out
Help Defense
Hustle

Head up

You have to have your head up and see the court when you're playing basketball. This is hard for some players to do because they can't dribble the ball well enough without having their head down and looking at the ball. When you are working on your ball handling drills, always work on them with your head up. Get used to dribbling and fending off defensive pressure with your head up so you can see your teammates and get them the ball quickly when they're open.

Hands out/Help defense

Active hands are very important on defense. When you're playing defense you need to have your arms and hands out and active in order to make it harder for the person you're guarding to pass the ball. "H" is also for "Help Defense." An important element of defense is to be able to guard your man and see where the ball is. When you see the ball, you will be able to step in and help if one of your teammates gets beat. If an opposing player that you are not guarding drives to the basket, you are responsible for helping out. You have to slide your feet quickly, leave the man that you're guarding, and move your body in front of the player that is driving to the basket.

Hustle

Hustle sums up a lot of what's already been talked about. It involves being assertive, anticipating the action, playing with high energy, getting back quickly on defense, always going to the ball, fighting through screens, playing hard defense, being willing to take on contact, and boxing out, just to name a few. All of these important parts of basketball can be summed up by coaches when talking about a player in four words, "he's a great hustler." You will hear players that are great hustlers also referred to as "having a great motor." Always give your all in everything you do. In order to be a great player you have to always hustle.

I

Intensity
IQ
Improvement

Intensity

Playing with intensity is incredibly important. Basketball is an intense game, period. Intensity means bringing energy, excitement, pride, determination, and spirit onto the floor with you every time you play. Dive for loose balls, draw charging fouls, and talk to your teammates. Play with heart. Be intense!

IQ

IQ is short for intelligence quotient and refers to how smart you are. In this case we're talking about having a high basketball IQ. You hear the term used in basketball a lot, as in: "That player has a high basketball IQ." To be that player, you have to always listen closely to your coach or you'll miss the little things that make a difference. Don't be looking around the gym or down at your sneakers when your coach is talking. Always make eye contact with your coach and concentrate on listening and comprehending what he or she is saying. When practice is over, think about your plays and what was said. Think about the defensive schemes you learned as well as the out of bounds plays, the zone plays and the man to man plays, *all of it*! There's a lot to think about, so do it in your spare time, outside of practice. Go over everything in your mind. Write things down and sketch out plays. The mental aspect of the game can never be taken lightly. Be the player that, not only knows everything he or she should be doing, but can also tell other players what they should be doing. Be a coach on the floor. To be great at anything requires thinking about it a lot. Basketball is no exception. You have to really work on it, so it can be said that you are a player that has a high basketball IQ!

Improvement

As you work on putting into practice everything you are learning through *The A-Z Basketball Book* understand that you will improve, but maybe not as quickly (or at the times) you would like. Improvement is a gradual thing and there will be times when you may feel you aren't even improving at all. That can be frustrating when you're working so hard at the sport. Quite often it happens that progress is not noticeable at all for a while and has seemed to flat line. Hang in there because, if you are disciplined with your commitment to basketball, there is usually a huge sudden leap of improvement with your game. Improvement is a not a straight line to the top. Understand that it will come and go in spurts.

J

Jumping
Jump shot

Jumping

You have to work on increasing how high you can jump. If you do jumping exercises and work on your leg strength, you will increase your jumping ability. Be sure to include jumping into your workout routine and check online for many training exercises and advice on how to improve your vertical leap. The ability to jump high no doubt helps you to become a better basketball player.

Jump shot

Jumping as high as you can and then shooting above your head is crucial in order to play good basketball. You first need to learn the fundamentals of shooting by practicing set shots as demonstrated on my website. From there, you can move on to shooting jump shots. Start very close to the basket when you work on your jump shot. You want to release the ball just before you reach the top of your jump. You don't want to release the ball at the very top of your jump or you will lose power. If you shoot it on your way up, it will be awkward and probably have too much power. Shoot just before you hit the peak of your jump. Keep your balance and work on making it feel comfortable by shooting lots of repetitions.

K

Knowledge of the game

Knowledge of the game

The fact that you are reading this book shows that you understand that it's extremely important to constantly gain knowledge about the game. You will never stop learning. That applies to everything in life, and basketball is no exception. You always have to be willing to learn, no matter how good you are or how much you think you know. Always seek knowledge and think of yourself as a knowledge seeker. Study the game on TV. Tape a game that you're watching for fun, so when it's over you can watch it back with the intent of studying it and learning from it. Study player's moves, plays, clock management, coaching strategies, and pick and roll execution. Pay particular attention to what players are doing when they don't have the ball, because when you watch a game for fun you tend to always watch the ball. What the other four players are doing, when they don't have the ball, is extremely important. There's always something new to learn. So keep your mind open and understand that, as a knowledge seeker you will never stop learning.

L

Love for the Game
Leadership

Love for the game

You have to love the game. I'm sure you do because it is an incredibly fun and exciting sport. However, your love for the game will be tested when you really commit to the hard work and dedication needed to be great. Getting up for a run or a workout on a cold morning, when you don't feel like it, will not seem like fun. This doesn't mean you no longer like the game. You don't realize it now because of how young you are, but it is a little like marriage. Through the years marriage isn't always fun and you will have tough times and have to work at getting through the rough patches. That doesn't mean you stop loving the person-or in this case the sport of basketball. This is where commitment and faith come in. You have to see it through and soon the love you seem to doubt will come shining through very brightly! Eventually, your love for basketball will also spill over into loving the PROCESS of becoming great-the hard work, commitment, dedication, and everything else that's required to achieve greatness. So while you may feel that you love the game now, know that at some point on your journey you will have rough patches. You have to stay committed and keep the faith! It's the only way.

Leadership

There's a lot of discussion of whether people are born with leadership skills or whether they can be learned. The answer is that it is always a little of both. There are some people that are born leaders and others that are naturally quiet and reserved, and are not so willing to speak up and lead. Maybe you don't think of yourself as a "rah, rah" kind of person and would rather not take on that responsibility. The truth is, if you practice all that is taught in this book, others will look up to you. You will be a natural leader because you are setting the proper example for others to follow. If you have strong character, confidence, commitment, and work very hard at improving your game, and you listen intently to the coach, and do all of the other things necessary to be great, others will look up to you and see you as a leader. It's important to know that you can be a leader without always having to be vocal. There are, however, effective leaders that are very loud and vocal, too. The point is that there are many different types of leadership styles. The fact that you want the best for you and your team, and you are always striving to do the right thing, you are a leader. Think of yourself as a leader! Maybe you do already; it's great if you do. Wherever you are with fulfilling a role as a leader, you should take on more of the responsibility to always keep your eyes and ears open and look for opportunities to continually practice and improve your current leadership skills. The world is in need of great leaders; your basketball team is too!

M

Moves
Move without the Ball
Mistakes
Motivation

Moves

There are a lot of moves to master to become great at basketball and it's been really interesting for me to watch them evolve through the years. All of the moves need to be practiced going both ways with each hand. Whatever move you do one way, needs to be practiced going the other way. This is why perfecting your ball handling is extremely important. If you can't dribble the ball really well with both hands you will not be able to learn all the moves necessary to be great. Check out A-ZBasketballBook.com to learn lots of moves. Also study players on TV and have fun practicing moves in your driveway. Several different moves can be combined and mixed and matched, so have fun with it. Hopefully, someday soon, a young kid somewhere will be in their driveway practicing your moves!

Move without the ball

In basketball there are always 10 players on the court and only one ball. What you do when you don't have the ball is very important. When you're on offense, your movement off the ball is crucial to your team's success. Basketball is a game of movement, so move! You should never be standing still watching the action. So what should you do when you don't have the ball? First, you should always have good floor balance. That means you and your teammates should be spread out on the court with good spacing between you. You should always be aware of where you are on the court and practice your leadership skills by helping and directing your teammates to where they should be. So, if you already have proper spacing on the court (floor balance) and you don't have the ball (you're off the ball), what should you do? Here are your options: 1) Set a screen for your teammate that has the ball (on ball screen). 2) Set a screen for a teammate that's away from the ball (screen away). 3) Cut through the lane and rotate away to let another player move toward the ball (cut through and go away). 4) Be ready to anticipate a shot so you can start boxing out your opponent and grab a rebound. There is always a way to move that will help your team when you don't have the ball.

Mistakes

Mistakes are a fact of life and are also a very big part of basketball. They will happen. What is very important is to learn from them and to try to not make the same mistakes over and over again. It's been said that, in every failure, is the seed of success. Failures and mistakes are not permanent. They are a great tool to use to learn to do things right. They will bring you closer to your goal. Don't beat yourself up over them! Get on with it, and go on to the next play and make sure you learned something from your error. Way too many coaches in youth basketball have their players so scared about making a mistake that they can't even play. It's a shame to see this because players need to be confident and loose and have fun with the game. You can't play effectively when you are playing in fear of making a mistake. Always think about all the great things you are going to do in the game and focus on that. When mistakes happen, what's important is that you play through them and learn from them.

Motivation

What motivates you to want to achieve greatness at basketball? It's a very noble pursuit to strive towards greatness at anything, but it's important to reflect on what it is that is motivating you. You may have been encouraged by your parents to start playing, or maybe you did it just because all your friends were playing. No matter what got you into the sport, the only thing that will keep you striving toward high achievement is your own self-motivation. You have to do it and want to do it. No one is going to do it for you and you shouldn't be playing it because someone else wants you to. It's all up to you! Most people have the desire to do something of significance with their lives, but many either lack the knowledge of how to achieve at a high level, or lack the motivation. They just aren't willing to do what it takes to achieve success. You are seeking the knowledge to attain greatness at basketball. The question then becomes: will you be self-motivated enough to propel yourself towards greatness?

<u>N</u>

Never give up
Nose for the ball
Next play

Never Give Up

The great North Carolina State coach Jimmy Valvano, while dying of cancer, gave in my opinion one of the greatest speeches in history at the first Excellence in Sports Performance Yearly Award (ESPY), presented by ESPN. If you have not seen it yet, I encourage you to go onto YouTube and take the time to watch and listen to it. It's one of the greatest displays of courage that I have ever seen and I still to this day, take the time to watch it when I'm in need of inspiration. His main message was this: "don't give up, don't ever give up." Throughout his fight with cancer, he never did. When faced with adversity, there will be times when you feel like giving up. If you're going to be great at the sport, giving up just isn't an option. Keep your dreams alive, always fight through adversity, and "don't give up, don't ever give up."

Nose for the ball

The message behind having a "nose for the ball" is similar to "go to the ball." The difference is that, if you have a "nose for the ball," you don't have to be told to "go to the ball." It's already instinctual and you're the player that coaches love because, wherever the ball is, you always seem to be there with your hands on it, or at least trying to get your hands on it. You always hustle. You never stand and watch someone else get a rebound, or just watch as your teammates scramble to save a ball from going out of bounds. You automatically go to the ball when it is passed to you and fight hard for loose balls because you have "a nose for the ball." You should be motivated to want to become the player that coaches say has a nose for the ball. Always hustle and think "anticipate" and "go to the ball," and hopefully your coaches will soon be saying that YOU have a great nose for the ball!

Next play

You already know that mistakes are a part of life and a part of basketball. You know that it's important to learn from them so you can keep them from being repeated in the future. "Next play" refers to the mindset that you need to have when you make a mistake. Quickly get over your mistake and think, "next play." Play on and maintain your great attitude both mentally, as well as in your strong confident body language. Maintain your composure and get on with the next play. Do not compound your error by not getting back on defense or standing there arguing a call. After a mistake always think, "next play."

O

Offense
Old School

Offense

There are many different offenses. The offensive plays you will learn and run are dependent on the players on your team and what your coach thinks is best. As a knowledge seeker and a person that is always looking to increase your basketball IQ, you will have no trouble understanding what to do on offense. Be sure to study your role within your team's offense when you are not at practice, and be willing to learn more than just your position. Work to understand the entire offense and what all your teammates need to do within the offense. That way you can practice being a leader by helping others to understand what they need to do. Get to the point where you understand the offense so well that you feel comfortable and can be more fluid within it. Too many young players are robotic with their movements because they have to think too hard about what to do and where to go. Offenses exist to try to give your team a high percentage chance of scoring a basket. This can oftentimes be accomplished easily by breaking away from the offense at the right time and improvising. In time, you will know when to take advantage of these situations within the flow of your offense. If, however, you are the player that is not comfortable with the offense and too often breaks away from it to get your shot, you will be sitting on the bench watching your teammates play. Learn your teams offense and know it inside and out, so that your coach will have the confidence in you to once in a while improvise from it, when you feel the time is right to get an easy score.

Old school

Never discount old-school basketball. Some of the greatest basketball was played by the Los Angeles Lakers and the Boston Celtics in the 1980s. Some of the best teamwork ever, along with astonishing fundamental basketball, has taken place in the past. And just like with the world of music, the songs and the artists may not be new and popular, but some of the best happened long ago. Never discount the past. Learn your history and understand where our country and the sport of basketball have come from. Only fools think because something is new it's better. There is no question that the game is evolving, along with training devices and methods, but that doesn't mean it's better. Be willing to learn something from the great players and teams that have gone before you. Go back and watch Lakers vs. Celtics play-off games from the '80s every chance you get, because there is unquestionably something to be learned.

P

Points
Pride
Passing
Practicing
Pick and Roll
Preparation
Process

Points

Points are the most obvious thing that determine the outcome of a basketball game. There are also a number of other things that need to happen on the court in order for your team to win. Not everyone is a scorer. If you are already a good scorer, then make sure you work extremely hard on all the other parts of the game. Work very hard at rebounding, passing, playing good defense, getting back on defense, moving without the ball, setting good screens, and being unselfish. These are just a few of the many things that go into winning a basketball game. Points are important. That's what most people notice during a game and they ultimately determine who wins and who loses a game. However, understand that there are many, many other things that go into making a successful player and a successful team. If you also work very hard on all the other parts of the game you will be well on your way to becoming a great player.

Pride

Have pride in yourself and what you do, but don't be boisterous. There's nothing worse than false pride. You will feel good about yourself when you set goals and strive to reach them. You will be confident in yourself because you are doing the right things. You deserve to be proud of yourself and carry yourself with pride; but you should refrain from talking about yourself and your accomplishments. This is more typically known as bragging. If your accomplishments are deserving of praise, then others will do it for you. Have pride in yourself and your achievements, but let others do the bragging for you. Also, take pride in how you approach all the other parts of the game besides scoring. Pride yourself on playing great defense. Pride yourself on being a great passer, a great rebounder, or a great hustler. Have pride in yourself and in your game but be humble.

Passing

It's very important to become a great passer. The only way to become a great passer is to become a great ball handler who always dribbles with your head up so you can see the court and your open teammates. Passes oftentimes have to happen very suddenly and quickly. Go to A-ZBasketballBook.com to learn many different passes and drills that will help you to become a better passer.

Practicing

Of course you've heard the saying, "Practice makes perfect." I'm not so sure there is a "perfect," but if you're going to work on getting close to perfect, you have to practice things the correct way. This is where the fundamentals come in. You have to practice the fundamentals of basketball in the right way to be able to achieve greatness. If you're practicing the fundamentals incorrectly, you can practice for hours and not get anywhere. My website, A-ZBasketballBook.com is there to help you understand the proper way to practice the fundamentals. Please make use of it! Yes, practice will make you great, but only if you practice the correct things in the correct way.

Pick and roll

The pick and roll is the most basic and effective play in all of basketball. It takes a lot of practice and a lot of time to perfect the pick and roll. When executed correctly, it is very difficult to stop. At its core, it is very basic. A screen needs to be set on the opposing player and then the player that sets the screen rolls to the basket to receive a pass for a layup. It's difficult to help you understand what to do in words. You need to go to my website to get a visual example on many things that are discussed in this book, including the pick and roll. When you are playing basketball with your friends-two on two or three on three-always work on executing the pick and roll. Like anything, the more you do it the better you will get at it.

Preparation/Process

The great Green Bay Packer's coach Vince Lombardi is quoted as saying, "The will to win is not nearly as important as the will to prepare to win." This is a very meaningful quote to ponder. Lombardi is saying that it's more crucial to have the will to commit to training and working out and learning fundamentals, than it is to be determined to win while a game is going on. Of course, it's very important to have a strong will to win when the game is going on, but if you haven't trained properly leading up to the game, the strongest will in the world will not get lesser skilled players the victory. Setting goals and being disciplined and committed to preparing to win-the process-is how to achieve greatness. I mentioned in my introduction that you have to love the process of working towards greatness. That is the secret that anyone who has ever achieved greatness in anything knows. Vince Lombardi knew it, and he shared his wisdom with the world in that one simple quote. Set goals, train hard, commit, stay focused, be disciplined-love the process of preparing to win and victory will be yours!

Q

Quality not quantity
Quickness

Quality not quantity

You already know how important practice is, and as emphasized earlier, practicing the right things in the correct manner makes all the difference. You have to remember that quality wins out over quantity every time. It's better to do a few drills or a few shots correctly, than it is to do many of them incorrectly. As you're practicing and working on all the different elements of the game, always remember to focus on quality.

Quickness

I'll refer to "speed" as being able to get from point A to point B as fast as possible. Quickness is about being able to stop and then go in another direction very fast. While playing basketball your feet constantly move and change direction very quickly, very often. This is referred to by many as "foot speed." (In this book, foot speed refers to "quick feet" or "quickness," and "speed," the ability to run fast, is covered under the letter "S.") Success with basketball requires both speed and quickness.

It's important to not only have quick feet but also quick hands. There are many footwork drills that will help improve your quickness. On the website A-ZBasketballBook.com there are exercises for you to work on. Arm and hand quickness can be improved by doing clap pushups and by hitting a speed bag. Speed bags are used by boxers. They are relatively inexpensive and can be hung up in your garage. A lot of coordination drills using a basketball also help to improve your arm and hand quickness and coordination. Many of those drills are also on the A-ZBasketballBook.com website. Having quick hands and feet are extremely important in basketball.

<u>R</u>

Rebounding

Role

Repetition

Rest and recovery

Resilience

Responsibility

Respect

Rebounding

The steps to rebounding have already been covered in the "Bs" with "boxing out," but it's such an important part of basketball that I chose to talk about it again. You can't be a good rebounder unless you learn to box out. And when you do learn to box out, you still won't be a good rebounder unless you possess the same traits needed to be a good defender. These traits were covered in the "Ds"-determination, dedication and discipline. Remember to hustle and be sure to grab the ball with two hands. Have a nose for the ball; be tough and take pride in the fact that you are great rebounder. It's a battle under the boards and you need to be assertive and impose your will onto your opponent. Do not be afraid of taking on contact. You can be a warrior and a great rebounder no matter what your size is.

Role

Every player on every team will play a role. Different players will be better at different parts of the game and so that's what they are expected to focus on. There are players whose role it is to be primarily a rebounder or defender, a ball-handler, or a shooter. The team whose players accept their role and work together as a team, are oftentimes a winning team. All-around players are those rare players that can do it all and those are the exceptional players. Not everyone can be that player.

You can still be a great player and serve a role on your team, even if you are not an all-round player. It can sometimes be hard for players to accept their role. Even though you think you should be on the starting five, maybe your coach likes the energy you bring to the game coming off the bench. Or maybe you feel you can shoot pretty well, but there are other players pegged as the shooters on the team and therefore get more shots than you do. You will need to come to terms with your role on your team. You may not like it, but you need to accept it and embrace it. Continue to work hard at improving yourself in all areas of the game, because things will change from year to year. If you want to be part of a winning team, you will need to work hard at fulfilling the role your coach has for you on this year's team. Next year maybe your role will change.

Repetition

I explained earlier how practicing the right things in the right way (quality) will help you improve your game and get you closer to becoming the great player you hope to become. There has to be repetition with anything in order to become great at it. Whether it's music, acting, studying, or in this case basketball, the correct things need to be repeated over and over again. This can be difficult because it may get monotonous or boring for you. You absolutely have to find joy in repeating the right things in the right way, over and over again, in order to achieve greatness at anything. Repetition is the key to unlocking the door to becoming a great basketball player.

Rest and recovery

As important as it is to repeat the right things in the right way, and to work hard at it, it is just as important to understand that your body needs rest and needs time to recover from being overworked. Take a little time to get away from the game once in a while, especially in the off-season. This will help recharge your batteries and enable you to come back mentally sharp, focused, and excited about the game.

Resilience

Being resilient is the ability to get knocked down and then to come back stronger than ever. Being resilient is a great life quality to have and it will also serve you well in basketball. There are many times that you will need to overcome adversity. You will make mistakes and have setbacks and you need to be able to get over them quickly and go onto the next play. This is referred to as resilience. Great players are all resilient players.

Responsibility

Being responsible doesn't mean you have to feel like you are wearing a ball and chain around your ankles. Many young people seem to work hard to avoid responsibility. Lots of adults also have this same mentality. Being a responsible person should make you feel proud and confident and will also help you to continue to build on your strong moral character. Being responsible will also help you feel worthy of being a leader. Help your caregivers out around the house. Do chores without being asked. Work hard at school. Be disciplined to do the right things on and off the basketball court. You are responsible. We are all responsible. It doesn't mean we can't feel free, enjoy ourselves, and have fun in life. It's quite the opposite. When we are responsible, we are proud and enjoy our lives more and feel more freedom. We are honoring the life we've been given and those that have gone before us by accepting responsibility and making a contribution. You have a responsibility to your country, school, parents, coach, teammates, but most importantly, to yourself! Embrace being responsible for your life and you will feel proud and free. All great people in life know the importance of being responsible. As Winston Churchill put it, "The cost of greatness is responsibility."

Respect

When you are a responsible person, you will have respect for yourself and therefore be able to respect others. A catchphrase that seems to be popular with teens lately is, "He was disrespecting me!" I have noticed that it was usually uttered by someone who looks like they had absolutely no respect for himself or herself to begin with. When you are doing the right thing and being responsible, you will have respect for yourself. You need to love who you are, respect yourself, and be your own best friend. It's then much easier to give others the respect they deserve. Respect your parents and your coaches. Respect your elders, your teachers, and your teammates. Also respect the game and those that have gone before you. Be responsible and always show respect.

S

Shooting
Student of the game
Screening
Steals
Speed

Shooting

The fundamentals of shooting are covered on my website. There is a textbook way to approach the art of shooting. It's usually stressed that all the different factors that go into proper shooting should be done a certain specific way. Elbow in, eyes on the target, bend your knees, square up to the basket, and many other details. While it's important to strive for perfection and work on shooting the correct way, it's important to note that many very good shooters have their own quirks that go against the conventional wisdom. This is not to say that you want to purposefully NOT shoot how you're supposed to shoot, or practice some unconventional shooting style, just because it works for a particular player. As a coach it has been my experience that if you are dedicated and committed to working on becoming a great shooter, you will probably, at some point, incorporate your own personality and style into your shot. Always practice shooting the right way with lots and lots of repetition.

Student of the game

When you love the game of basketball and are truly a knowledge seeker and are self-motivated to do what's necessary to become a great player, you have become a student of the game. A student of the game is a player who works on understanding their team's offense, studies games both present and past, and is always open to learning. A student of the game has learned the rules and accepts responsibility and works towards having a high basketball IQ. Very few players can be called "a student of the game." All the great ones can.

Screening

Screening is also referred to as setting a pick. It's when you stand wide and strong, and put your body in the way of an opposing player to help a teammate to get open. You have to not be moving as you set a screen and you cannot be afraid of taking on a little contact. If a teammate is coming to set a screen for you, be sure to not move until your teammate has planted a solid screen. If you screen on the ball and then roll off of the screen, this is referred to as a pick and roll. As mentioned earlier the pick and roll is a highly effective play and is demonstrated for you on my website. Be willing to set hard screens. It won't show up in the box score but good screens can certainly determine the outcome of a basketball game.

Steals

Steals are the result of playing great defense, anticipating the action, and having quick feet and hands. Steals are great, but you want to be sure to not gamble on trying to get a steal too often. Trying to get a steal from your defender can result in unnecessary fouls or allow your opponent to get between you and the basket, giving the opposing team an advantage. This is all because you chose to go for the steal. You have to pick your spots carefully. The majority of the time it's best to just play straight up, hard-nosed defense. If your team is losing and it's getting late in the game, it may be necessary to take more of a chance and jump the passing lane (go for the steal when the ball is being passed to the person you're guarding) or flat out just try to strip the ball. You will know when the time is right to take a chance, but you don't want to do it if too often you're coming up empty-handed and leaving your team at a disadvantage. That's a sure way to get you a seat on the bench. Get most of your steals from being tough on defense and having quick and active hands and feet, and not too many from unnecessary gambling.

Speed

Speed is how fast you can run. You already know that it's important to make running sprints part of your workout routine. Getting from one end of the floor to the other very fast is a great skill to have. What is important to know concerning speed is that the majority of the time you are on the court, you need to vary your speed. You don't want to run 100 miles per hour every minute you're on the court. When your team loses possession, yes you need to sprint back on defense. You also want to get down the court fast when your team is running the fast break. When running your offense you need to understand that you should not always be moving at top speed. You want to change your speed and change your direction often when playing basketball. Go medium speed, then slow speed, and then accelerate fast. Mix up your speed. This applies to when you're on the ball, as well as off the ball. Don't show off all your speed, all the time. Be sure to vary your speed and keep your opponent guessing. Remember, change of speed and change of direction!

T

Toughness
Triple threat
Talk
Team player
Teamwork

Toughness

When people think of toughness they think of the big and brawny bully shoving people around and calling people names. This isn't what being tough in basketball is all about. Toughness is about meeting and accepting all the challenges put forth in this book. It's much more mental than physical. It's about doing the right things and accepting responsibility for yourself and your actions. It's understanding that it's the process that's important and having the discipline to prepare to win that makes real winners. It's about having the courage to set goals, believe in them, and to have faith in yourself. Trash talking on the court isn't being tough. Being tough is hustling for loose balls, playing with intensity, quickly playing through mistakes, and being an unselfish team player. Being tough is having a fighter mentality, while pushing yourself further than what you thought was possible. Working hard and setting an example for others to follow is being tough. Being responsible and respectful is being tough. Any thug can push people around and call people names. To really be tough is reserved for those who are great.

Triple Threat

When you're in an athletic position, slightly bent over at the waist, with your knees bent, and your hands out, you are in what's called the triple threat position. You are able to do three things immediately if someone passes you the ball. You can 1) shoot, 2) pass, and 3) dribble. Always be sure to look to shoot, if you are in good range, or quickly pass to a teammate that is in a better position than you are. You can only do these two things quickly if you are in an athletic triple threat position. Do not use dribbling as your first option. You should only dribble if you have a clear lane to the basket for an easy score. Save your dribble and look first to pass or shoot. If these are not options, then use your dribble. But while you're using your dribble, be sure to be thinking about the only two options left-shooting or passing. Try not to stop dribbling until you've executed a pass or a shot. When looking to receive a pass, always be in the triple threat position, so you can react quickly and use any of your three options. But remember; don't waste your dribble right away, unless you have a clear lane to the basket.

Talk (communicate)
Great players talk it up in basketball. It helps to keep you and your teammates focused on the court. You should talk to give encouragement, compliments, and reminders to your teammates about game situations. Communication is extremely important in basketball. It's also an easy opportunity for you to practice leadership skills.

All of the following are examples of things that can be said to help your team during a game:

- "SHOT" (yell this when you see a shot go up or about to go up)
- "#12 is a shooter"
- "Don't forget he's a lefty, force him right"
- "I got ball"
- "Great hustle"
- "Don't worry about it, shake it off"
- "Don't forget we're pressing after a made basket"
- "Play tough"
- "Nice pass"
- "Let's get a stop on this one guys"
- "I've got #32"
- "Nice job"
- "Find your man"
- "We don't have any more timeouts"
- "Screen right"
- "We're still in man to man"

The list goes on and on. Team players always take the initiative to talk it up on the court. It will not only help you, but it will also help your team and coaches love the great players that communicate. It's also important to talk with your coach about anything you don't understand or when you want better clarification concerning your role on the team or any other issues.

Team player/Teamwork

For a team to be successful there needs to be teamwork. Having great teamwork means that all the players on the team are team players; starting with you. An effective team player understands their role and will do what's necessary for the good of the team. If all the players on a team have this mindset, there will be effective teamwork. Teamwork is a very powerful force. Throughout history, the majority of wins and the most successful teams play with great teamwork.

U

Unselfishness
Understand your coach

Unselfishness

You already know it's important to be unselfish. This quality was covered quite extensively under "assist", along with the importance of understanding the universal law of giving. This law is, "when you give you get." The concept of being unselfish is so important in the game of basketball, it needs to be emphasized one more time. For a team to be a great team, its players need to be concerned with having great teamwork. In order for this to happen, the team must have unselfish players. Selfish players ruin team chemistry, team spirit, and ultimately lead to team failure. Unselfish players are aware that in basketball, as in life, it's necessary to step outside of ourselves and our self-serving motivations for the betterment of the team. Understanding this means you, and everyone around you, will be more successful. You will get what you desire. You will be a winner and also help to make your teammates winners as well. As you give you get.

Understand your coach

You may not always agree with or understand the motivation of your coach, but it's important to try. The coach has the final say in matters concerning the team and it's not always easy to make tough decisions. If something is really eating at you concerning your role on the team, or why certain things are done the way they are, you need to talk to your coach. It can be difficult for young players to open up and talk to their coach, but be responsible and do it! Get things off your chest! It will help you to understand your coach better. You may still disagree but you're going to have to live with the coach's decision and play on. At least you will have talked, and opened the communication lines. You're working at trying to understand your coach's style and philosophy. Again, you may not always see eye to eye, but if you want to be a successful player on a successful team, you're going to need to accept your coach's way of doing things and work hard at being the best team player you are capable of becoming.

V

Vision
Visualize

Vision

Vision means having good court vision. Being aware of everyone on the court and everything that's taking place. When you have good court vision you are always dribbling with your head up and can see your teammates at all times. Not only can you see your own teammates, but you are very aware of all the opposing players too. A player with good court vision can see the movement of all players, and can anticipate what they are going to do and where they are going to go. To have good court vision takes practice and time. You have to start with first becoming a great ball handler and get to the point where you never have to look at the ball when you're dribbling. After that, you have to be an unselfish team player. Really get to know your teammates and their tendencies on the court. Then you just have to play the game. Like anything in life, you can't get good at something without doing it over and over again. Be conscious of possessing good court vision-it's a must for all great players!

Visualize

A mind can be an anxious and restless thing. It's often difficult to remain focused and in the present moment. This uneasiness has been referred to as "the mad monkey of the mind." This "mad monkey" takes us out of the moment and often runs wild telling us things such as, "don't miss this shot," or "what if I'm not good enough," or other negative thoughts that are not productive. Most uneasiness is rooted in the fear of failure. The negative mindset needs to be overcome in order to be a great player. This can be accomplished by proper visualization. You need to visualize what you want to have happen, and see and think nothing else. Keep negative thoughts such as, "I can't miss this free throw" or "I can't make a mistake here" completely out of your mind. Instead, focus on the positive. Visualize what you want to happen and see yourself making that happen. Be confident. You've put your hard work in and have been doing the right things. You deserve for great things to happen. Visualize yourself doing just that and become the great player that you envision. Visualization is a very powerful tool used by all great players. Always work to stay focused and visualize what you want to have happen.

W

Weak hand
Working out
Winning

Weak hand

Weak hand falls under the category of becoming a good ball handler, but is important enough to be re-emphasized here in the "Ws." Everyone has a weak hand, and you have to start early and work hard at making it equal to your strong hand. You have to dribble, shoot, and pass with equal ability with both hands. Always work your weak hand (also called off hand) as much as possible. Many players don't put the time and effort into developing their weak hand properly, because it feels awkward. Instead, they just continue to play using their primary hand. This is a big mistake. You will not become great at basketball without developing your weak hand. Everything you do with your strong hand, make sure to do it with your weak hand.

Working out

A designated time that you set aside to concentrate and work hard on a physical activity that will improve your game is called working out. There are many different things that you can work on, and you have to be disciplined and dedicated to make it all happen. If you want to be a great basketball player you have got to have a very strong work ethic. There are many drills on A-ZBasketballBook.com and there are many more that you can find elsewhere online. When you understand all that needs to be done to become a great player, it's up to you to put together the program that works best for you. Be sure to set specific days and times when you plan to work out, and stick with it. Also be sure to mix in a lot of play too. Shoot around for fun while still thinking about shooting the ball correctly. As you're shooting around, mix in under the basket hook layups, crossover dribbles, and lots of moves. Have fun with it!

All of the different workouts required to be a great athlete and player that have been discussed are grouped into daily areas of focus. They can be rotated from day to day and mixed and matched. Listen to your body and don't overwork yourself. Take time for rest and recovery. Take a few days off here and there. Remember that you can do exercises that involve only using your own body weight such as push-ups, chin-ups, sit-ups, and dips every day, with just a few days off here and there. Set goals as to how many you are going to do each day and stick with it. Remember measurable goals? You can also always work on shooting or dribbling as often as you want too. Exercises that stress the muscles out, such as lifting weights, require that you take days off to recover. You also want to be careful with lots of sprinting or jumping to make sure your knees and legs have time to recover. Lastly, you should know that eating the right foods is crucial. Eat a balanced diet with lots of fruits and vegetables and be sure to drink plenty of water. Cut down on soda and junk food. No one said it was going to be easy. If it were easy, everyone would be great. Greatness is reserved for just the few that learn what needs to be done, and go out and do it! Here is a sample grouping of things to work on each day:

1. Run sprints, do defensive work, skip rope, hit a speed bag (or do lots of clap pushups), play
2. Strength work, jogging, basketball coordination drills, play
3. Ball handling, passing, shooting, jumping, play

Winning

Winning is very similar to achievement in that it cannot be attained unless you are committed to the process and preparation that goes into being successful. Is all the information that you're learning sinking in? Are you committed and disciplined and making all this happen? Have you set measurable goals that will allow you to look back and reflect on how you are doing? Are you eating right, practicing gratitude, and keeping the faith? Are you a knowledge seeker and student of the game, working towards having a high basketball IQ? Are you unselfish, tough, and determined to do all of the little things necessary to be great at the game? Have you dedicated yourself to playing great defense and rebounding? Will you be resilient and able to overcome adversity when it arises? Will you always keep a great attitude and be an enthusiastic, confident, and respectful person? These are the things that go into making a great person, as well as a great player. Become the person that is always striving to do his or her best. Even then, you will be faced with losses throughout your basketball career. The great UCLA coach John Wooden summed up best what winning means when he said: "You always win when you make the full effort to do the best of what you're capable." So now you know what "winning" really is.

X

eXtra work
eXcuses

eXtra work

It goes without saying that, if you want to be the best at something, you have to put in a lot of extra work. After you've finished shooting around, working on your ball handling skills, or other parts of your game, and you feel you've done enough, do a little more. The stories of the great ones being the first player in the gym and the last player to leave are legendary. Larry Bird and Michael Jordan were two players that always went above and beyond what everyone else was doing. They understood that, if you want to be better than everyone, you have to get more reps in than everyone else. There's an old quote that's been around for a long time and it goes like this: "when you're not working on your game, someone else somewhere else is." You have to work very hard to be successful.

eXcuses

The people who fail in life are the people with lots of excuses. If you are courageous enough to commit to traveling the path of greatness, and I believe you are, then do it. Save your excuses. There are no excuses. Ben Franklin said, "He that is good at making excuses is seldom good for anything else." Be responsible and do not lower yourself by making excuses. If you do find yourself making an excuse, reflect on it and trace it back to try to understand where it came from. You can then learn from it and begin to understand how destructive excuses are. Work on eliminating them from your life. Great people and players have no time for excuses.

<u>Y</u>

You

You

"You" means that it all comes down to you. It's been said that a person can create a hell from heaven or a heaven from hell. Now that's getting a little philosophical, but what it means is that you create the world that you want to live in *with your mind*. It's all up to you. Having made it this far in the book, you should have a very good understanding of what it will take to achieve greatness. The ball is now in your hands. With so much information covered in this book I hope, as I mentioned in the introduction, that you will keep it handy and reread and refer to it often. It's a good idea to choose to reread any letter of the alphabet in any random order at your leisure. This will help keep the ideas, concepts, and motivations fresh in your mind as you continue on your path towards greatness. Drop me a line on my website and let me know how things are going. I wish you all the best. Before getting on with our last letter I'd like to leave you with one thing John Wooden felt was important for all of us to know and do and it's this; "Acquire peace of mind by making the effort to become the best of which YOU are capable".

Z

Zest for life

Zest for Life

"Z" stands for zest for life. Have a zest for life and bring that into everything you do. Also take some time to ponder this great quote from the philosopher Socrates, "The unexamined life is not worth living." You should always make time to sit quietly without any distractions and reflect on your life. Turn off the TV, cell phones, computers-all electronics, and reflect inward. Ponder where you've come from, and what path lies ahead. This is essential. When you set aside time to examine your life, you begin to know yourself better and you are able to take control of your life. You decide who you want to be, and can work toward becoming that person. If your goal is to be a great basketball player, then get on with it! Have a zest for life and always remember that it's what you learn after you know it all that counts!

###

Index

Steals, 76-77
Student of the game, 75-76

T
Talk, 81-83
Team player, 83
Teamwork, 83
Toughness, 80
Triple threat, 80-81

U
Understand your coach, 85-86
Unselfishness, 85

V
Vision, 88
Visualize, 88-89

W
Weak hand, 91
Winning, 93-94
Working out, 91-93

X
eXcuses, 96-97
eXtra work, 96

Y
You, 99

Z
Zest for life, 101

Lightning Source UK Ltd.
Milton Keynes UK
UKHW011313110520
363092UK00005B/712